THE HEYDAY OF
NINE ELMS
AND ITS
LOCOMOTIVES

COLIN BOOCOCK

First published 1992

ISBN 0 7110 2067 1

© Ian Allan Ltd 1992

Published by Ian Allan Ltd, Shepperton, Surrey; and
printed by Ian Allan Printing Ltd at their works at
Coombelands in Runnymede, England.

Front cover: Ivatt Class 2 2-6-2T No 41312
arrives at Clapham Junction with a train from
Kensington Olympia on 30 June 1967.
Alan Trickett

Back cover: Most steam depots found that
bottlenecks occurred at service points such as
the coal stage and the turntable. Rebuilt 'Battle
of Britain' 4-6-2 No 34052 *Lord Dowding* pulls
off Nine Elms' table after turning.
Malcolm Knight

Right: A premier Southern Railway locomotive
at the premier Southern depot: in April 1947,
'Merchant Navy' class Pacific No 21C11 *General
Steam Navigation* waits at the exit from Nine
Elms depot, with its fire being inexpertly made
up. *H. N. James/Colour-Rail*

IAN ALLAN
Publishing

Introduction

Steam sheds were fascinating. A great London passenger depot could reach the pinnacle of prestige in a young enthusiast's eyes.

Steam sheds were not the shiny, well-lit, oily-clean and programmed depots to which we have become accustomed in the modern traction age. They were dirty (always, but some more than most), often unkempt, smoky, dusty and quite hazardous places. The hub of human activity in a steam shed was the running foreman's office. Outside this, usually in a lobby, were posted the enginemen's rosters and locomotive workings for the day. On the Southern Railway, and later the Southern Region of British Railways, the engine's duty number was stencilled on one of its white headcode discs.

Nine Elms depot was strategically placed to serve Waterloo station, London's greatest terminus. Nine Elms, or 70A as it was coded by BR, supplied 'Merchant Navy' class locomotives for prestigious trains such as the 'Bournemouth Belle' and the 'Atlantic Coast Express'. The Southampton boat trains, among them the 'Cunarder', the 'Normandy Express' and the 'Brittany Express', might well have Nine Elms Pacific or 4-6-0 motive power. The summer Saturday trains to Lymington Pier ('Change for the Isle of Wight') had 'Schools' class 4-4-0s in the 1960s.

Even if a train arrived at Waterloo hauled by an engine based elsewhere, it had to go to Nine Elms for turning, coaling, watering and servicing. Thus,

Bournemouth 'West Country' Pacifics off the 'Royal Wessex' were to be seen among the engines queuing for Nine Elms' coaling plant. A Salisbury 'first batch' 'Merchant Navy' class 4-6-2 often stood in the yard adorned with 'Devon Belle' plates.

There were lesser engines to be seen at Nine Elms, too. The local trains, which called at all stations along the main line from Woking to Basingstoke, used older motive power: 'T14' 'Paddlebox' 4-6-0s; 'Remembrances'; 'King Arthurs'; 'H15s'; even, 'T9' 4-4-0s were common in the early 1950s. The next decade brought in 'Schools' class 4-4-0s and BR Standard '4' and '5' 4-6-0s to these semi-fast workings.

Then there were the locomotives which took the empty stock trains to and from Clapham Junction carriage sheds. All Waterloo main line steam-hauled trains, bar one, visited Clapham between trips. Many needed remarshalling. The modern method, whereby standard formations are reversed in the terminus, just did not apply in those days. The 13 green coaches for a down Bournemouth train might arrive at Waterloo behind a malachite green or black 'M7' 0-4-4T. In later years a former GWR 0-6-0 pannier tank might be used for the empty stock, or a BR Standard '3' 2-6-2T. On departure, the tank engines would bank heavy trains to the outer end of the platform to give them a good start. For a time, the Pullman coaches of the 'Bournemouth Belle' were serviced at Stewart's Lane depot.

There was not much freight to be hauled by Nine Elms locomotives. On the Western Section of the Southern Region, Feltham was the London-end depot for heavy freight engines. The occasional Woolwich 'Mogul' or '700' class, 'Q' or 'Q1' 0-6-0 might be seen at Nine Elms on the coal trains for the coaling plant. Urie's heavy 4-8-0T or 4-6-2T engines appeared on occasions.

The main line was really the only purpose for Nine Elms depot's later existence. All branch lines off the main line beyond Clapham Junction as far west as Brookwood had been electrified by the Southern Railway in the interwar years or earlier. The steam trains represented glamour among the faceless, green, electric multiple-units, which thronged the tracks to Waterloo.

There were some unusual locomotives at Nine Elms from time to time. In 1951, the depot was host to 'Britannias' Nos 70009 *Alfred the Great* and 70014 *Iron Duke*; the former worked the 'Bournemouth Belle' roster for a season during the Festival of Britain. Between 1951 and 1954 the Southern's three 1Co-Co1 diesel-electrics, along with the ex-LMS twins Nos 10000 and 10001, worked Nine Elms' top turns until the five locomotives were transferred to the London Midland Region.

In 1953 'Merchant Navy' 4-6-2 No 35020 *Bibby Line* broke its crank axle while passing through Crewkerne station at speed — fortunately with no derailment. This potentially dangerous event caused all 30 'Merchant Navy' Pacifics to be withdrawn immediately for axle examination and replacement. Nine Elms received engines from other Regions to fill the gap. Thus came some 'Britannia' Pacifics from the Western Region, 'V2' 2-6-2s from the Eastern, and LMS and BR

Class 5 4-6-0s from the London Midland Region. The 'V2s' became favourites with Nine Elms crews and worked the 'Bournemouth Belle' for many weeks.

It isn't just the engine crews we should remember, even though they had many superb locomotive performances to their credit. Nine Elms engines were generally well maintained by the fitters and boilersmiths who attended them. The engines were normally well cleaned, except in the difficult last year or two. Yet other men at the depot had the difficult and soul-destroying tasks of raking out ashpans and firegrates, cleaning boiler flue tubes, brushing soot off firebox tubeplates or cleaning out smokeboxes. And someone had to pick up the ash and other debris from the depot floor and dispose of it.

Nonetheless, when the depot closed in 1967 it was with sadness that people watched the end of main line steam. For when the last Bulleid Pacific had arrived from Weymouth on 9 July 1967, and had been turned and despatched westwards for stabling, the railway had no need for Nine Elms depot any more. The site was later sold off, to become the centre for a large wholesale food market.

In its heyday Nine Elms had been the top depot, on Britain's last main line to use Pacific steam power on principal express trains. That makes 70A unique in British history.

Right: In May 1967, No 35023 *Holland-Afrika Line* stands amid the dirt and jumble which typified British steam locomotive depots.
C. M. Kapolka

Left: Steam locomotives, Bulleid Pacifics in particular, needed occasional use of sand on the rails to minimise wheelslip on greasy rails. The sandboxes of No 34002 *Salisbury* are filled at Nine Elms on 26 June 1966. Beware of getting sand on bearings! *G. S. Cocks*

Below: Very often, depot shunting was entrusted to a locomotive of ancient and rare lineage. In the depths of Nine Elms 'old shed' in April 1949 is former Plymouth, Devonport & South Western Junction 0-6-0T No 756 *A. S. Harris*. *T. B. Owen/Colour-Rail*

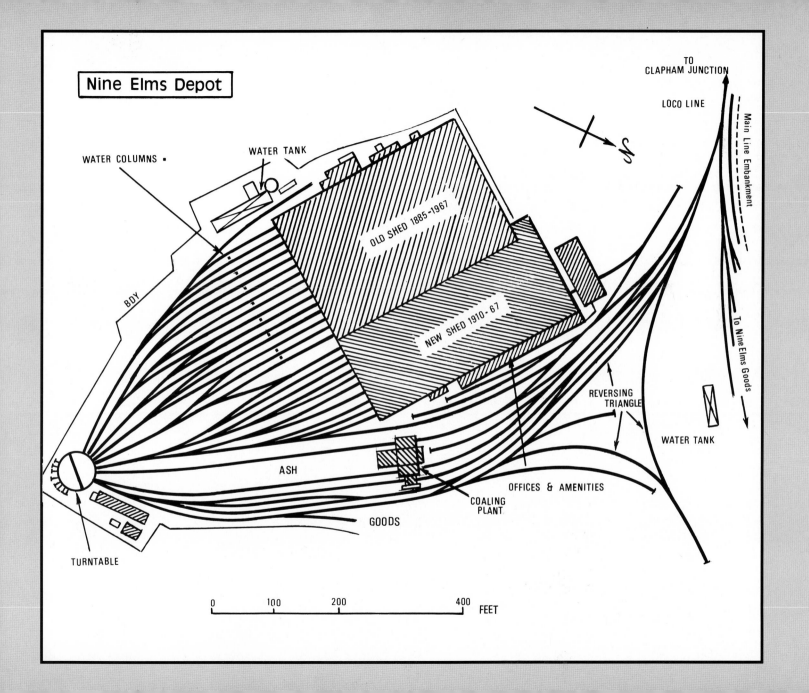

Nine Elms Depot

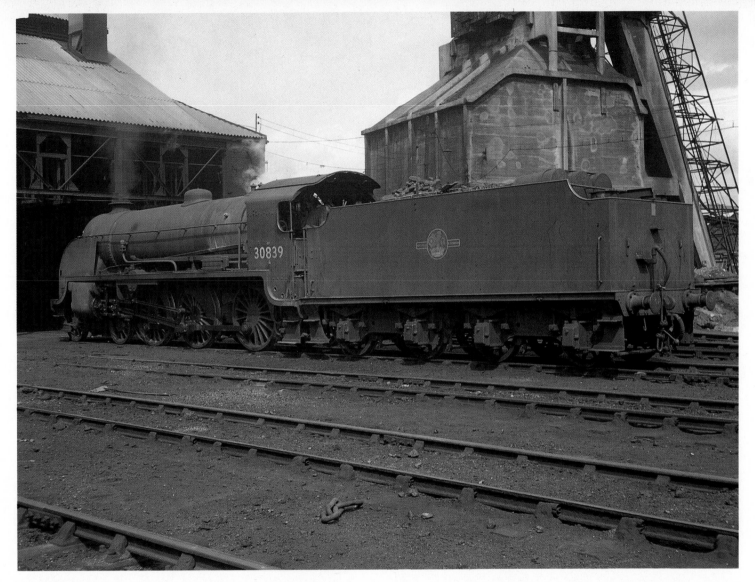

Left: Outside the 'old shed' stands a selection of locomotives which once would have been foreign to Nine Elms. Because of the closure of Bricklayers' Arms and other depots, 70A was host in May 1960 to ex-LB&SCR 'E4' 0-6-2T No 32498, a 'D1' 4-4-0 and two 'C' class 0-6-0s, including No 31510. *J. Oatway*

Above: The dominant colour around many steam depots was grey — the colour of coal dust and soot. Maunsell 'S15' 4-6-0 No 30839 stands outside Nine Elms 'new shed' in April 1965. *Geoff Rixon*

Above: Rebuilt Bulleid 'Battle of Britain' class 4-6-2 No 34052 *Lord Dowding* is prepared at Nine Elms depot for a special train duty. *Malcolm Knight*

Right: Nine Elms had some of Maunsell's fine 'Schools' class 4-4-0s for Bournemouth line workings before World War 2. It was only at the end of the 1950s that any of the 'Vs' returned there, when displaced from the South Eastern Division by Type 3 diesels. They worked Basingstoke and Salisbury stopping trains, as well as the summer Saturday Lymington boat trains. Here BR Standard 4-6-0 No 73118 *King Leodegrance* is flanked by 'Schools' Nos 30936 *Cranleigh* and 30902 *Wellington*. *G. W. Morrison*

Left: A close-up of the Walschaerts valve gear with outside admission piston valves as fitted to a rebuilt Bulleid Pacific as seen at Nine Elms in late 1963. *D. Herman*

Right: Rebuilt 'Merchant Navy' No 35019 *French Line CGT* simmers gently outside the old shed at Nine Elms. No 35019 was the penultimate 'Merchant Navy' to be constructed by the Southern Railway before Nationalisation and was rebuilt in May 1959. The locomotive was destined to be withdrawn in September 1965. *D. Herman*

Left: Rebuilt 'Merchant Navy' No 35015 *Rotterdam Lloyd* moves away from the turntable whilst 'Lord Nelson' No 30862 *Lord Collingwood* waits patiently to be turned. The coaling stage, prominent in the middle distance, was a typical feature of many of the more important loco sheds in the country and dated from the interwar years. *D. Herman*

Above: Rebuilt 'West Country' No 34025 *Whimple*, stands on the main through road north of the new shed. Rebuilt in 1957, *Whimple* was one of the Bulleid Pacifics which saw service through to the end of Southern Region steam in July 1967. The through road ran between the new shed and the coaling stage, the latter being situated to the left of the photographer. *D. Herman*

Left: A shot in late 1963 of Nine Elms shed sees rebuilt 'Merchant Navy' No 35007 *Aberdeen Commonwealth* blowing off outside the New Shed. Built as No 21C7 in June 1942, *Aberdeen Commonwealth* was to see its Silver Jubilee immediately prior to withdrawal in July 1967. *D. Herman*

Right: For most of the postwar life of the 'Bournemouth Belle' Pullman train Nine Elms supplied motive power in the form of 'Merchant Navy' class Pacifics, although occasionally Bulleid light Pacifics hauled this heavy train. Here, 'Merchant Navy' No 21C12 *United States Lines* passes Queen's Road, Battersea, in fine style in April 1947. *H. N. James/Colour-Rail*

Above: Many Southern railwaymen knew their 'Merchant Navy' class engines as 'Channel Packets' from the name of the first member of the class. No 35001 *Channel Packet* starts an up Weymouth-Waterloo express out of Bournemouth Central around 1960. *Colin Boocock*

Right: For many years empty stock workings between Waterloo and the carriage depot at Clapham Junction were entrusted to former London & South Western Railway Drummond 'M7' 0-4-4Ts, a class which had originally been allocated to Nine Elms for suburban workings prior to electrification. No 30249 plods past Vauxhall heavily laden in September 1962. *Colour-Rail*

SR and early BR

Left: All express locomotives from foreign depots visiting Waterloo were serviced at Nine Elms. Just prewar, in 1938, Urie 'N15' 4-6-0 No 739 *King Leodegrance* calls at Winchester with a Waterloo-Bournemouth train. *Colour-Rail*

Below left: Former L&SWR express engines such as the Drummond 'T14' 'Paddlebox' 4-6-0s found later use on stopping trains to Basingstoke and Salisbury. No 443 had just been set aside by June 1949 when seen at Nine Elms.
H. N. James/Colour-Rail

Right: Nine Elms was, for many years, the home depot of all the second batch of 10 'Merchant Navy' 4-6-2s. This is malachite green No 21C12 *United States Lines* at Nine Elms in April 1947.
N. N. James/Colour-Rail

Above: Nine Elms was hit by a German bomb during World War 2. Under the resultant hole in the roof stands malachite green 'N15' 'King Arthur' 4-6-0 No 774 *Sir Gaheris* in April 1947. *H. N. James/Colour-Rail*

Above: Some of the Nine Elms' 'M7' 0-4-4Ts, which were used for carriage shunting and which were therefore in the public eye at Waterloo, were painted malachite green even into BR days. No 30241 was so painted when seen at Nine Elms in May 1952. *T. B. Owen/Colour-Rail*

Above: Other locomotives associated with Nine Elms and Waterloo were the 'Lord Nelson' class. In March 1959 No 30857 *Lord Howe* stands ready to depart with the 11.30am semi-fast to Bournemouth.
D. C. Ovenden/Colour-Rail

Right: Bulleid's Southern Region diesel-electrics were employed on Nine Elms locomotive diagrams between 1951 and 1954. 2,000hp 1Co-Co1 No 10201 stands in Dorchester South station (where the up platform was reached by reversing off the main line) in May 1952 with the Weymouth portion of an express to Waterloo. *S. C. Townroe/Colour-Rail*

Below right: For a time the two LMS/LMR Co-Co diesels also worked 70A turns. No 10000 speeds near Shawford in 1954 with the down 'Royal Wessex' (4.35pm from Waterloo to Bournemouth, Swanage and Weymouth). *B. J. Swain/Colour-Rail*

Above: During the 1951 Festival of Britain, Nine Elms shed was host to two 'Britannia' class 4-6-2s. Of these, No 70009 *Alfred the Great* held to the 'Bournemouth Belle' roster for the summer of that year. No 70009 was photographed at Branksome depot, near Bournemouth.
S. C. Townroe/Colour-Rail

Right: The 70A-allocated rebuilt 'Merchant Navy' Pacific No 35018 *British India Line* waits to start a Bournemouth express train out of Waterloo on 2 December 1962. The small numerals '4' in the white destination code discs denote the Nine Elms duty number for that particular diagram. The position of the discs indicate a train for the Bournemouth line.
Brian Morrison

Waterloo terminus

Above: This view of the main line platforms at Waterloo in the afternoon sunshine on 31 March 1967 shows the usual row of Southern green EMUs, plus rebuilt 'West Country' 4-6-2 No 34004 *Yeovil. Alan Trickett*

Right: The empty coaches of the Bournemouth Belle are watched by an interested crowd as BR Class 4 2-6-4T No 80015 takes the Pullman stock away from Waterloo on 7 July 1967. *Douglas Hume*

Above: In July 1957 the first Bulleid 'West Country' light Pacific to be rebuilt, No 34005 *Barnstaple*, starts a Bournemouth line train out of Waterloo terminus. *B. J. Swain*

Right: Locomotives on empty stock duties often used the water crane at Waterloo. This Ivatt Class 2 2-6-2T No 41284 was originally built with vacuum push-pull equipment, but when reallocated to the Southern Region this was removed and straight standard steam pipes fitted. It was photographed at the terminus early in 1967. A set of Bournemouth line 'TC' electric trailer stock is in the background. *Alan Wild*

Above: Steam locomotive crews working in and out of Waterloo, indeed over most of the Southern, had to be careful of the live third-rails when walking round their locomotives with oil cans. 'Merchant Navy' class 4-6-2 No 35007 *Aberdeen Commonwealth* (now without its nameplates) had been prepared at Nine Elms depot before working the 'Dorset Limited' enthusiasts' special on 3 June 1967. Its sad exterior condition reflects the lack of cleaners taken on for work in the last years of steam operation on the Southern. *Alan Trickett*

The Road to the West

Right: No 35018 *British India Line* was one of Nine Elms' favourite express engines. On 1 August 1962 it awaits departure from Waterloo with the 'Atlantic Coast Express', a complex train which had portions to Ilfracombe, Padstow and Plymouth, as well as to some of the South Devon branches. *Les Elsey.*

Above: A Salisbury-bound semi-fast service potters along the slow road at Fleet on the Brookwood-Basingstoke four-track section, headed by 'West Country' light Pacific No 34002 *Salisbury* in the summer of 1964. The train contains an ex-LMS bogie van as well as Southern and BR stock.
B. J. Swain

Right: No 34023 *Blackmore Vale* comes out from under the Battledown flyover, which takes the up Bournemouth line over the West of England main line, with the 8.25am from Plymouth to Waterloo on 30 May 1964.
Hugh Ballantyne

Left: On 18 May 1964 rebuilt 'West Country' light Pacific No 34096 *Trevone* takes an evening West of England express past Worting Junction. *Rodney Lissenden*

Above: Maunsell 'N15' 4-6-0 No 30796 *Sir Donidas le Savage*, recently transferred from the Eastern Section of the Southern and still with its six-wheel tender, has a lightweight local train formed of a three-coach Bulleid set when seen approaching Battledown flyover from the west in April 1960. The headcode denotes the Waterloo-Exeter route. *P. J. Hughes/Colour-Rail*

Left: In September 1955 a similar local train was photographed leaving Salisbury tunnel behind a Maunsell 'S15' mixed traffic 4-6-0 No 30829. *B. J. Swain*

Right: Rebuilt 'Merchant Navy' 4-6-2 No 35022 *Holland America Line* was always a good performer. On 2 June 1963 it is leaving Salisbury on the up 'Atlantic Coast Express'. *Les Elsey*

Above: On 24 May 1963 'West Country' No 34002 *Salisbury* pauses at Templecombe with an up express. *Douglas Hume*

Right: Rebuilt 'Merchant Navy' 4-6-2 No 35025 *Brocklebank Line* pulls away from Yeovil Junction with an Exeter-Waterloo express on 20 October 1963. *Rodney Lissenden*

Left: No 34029 *Lundy* arrives at Exeter Central with a train from Waterloo. One of the 'E1/R' 0-6-2 radial tanks used for banking from Exeter St Davids stands in the middle road. *B. J. Swain*

Bournemouth and boat trains

Right: The pride of the Bournemouth line was its Pullman train, the 'Bournemouth Belle'. The down train is seen passing Esher headed by light Pacific No 34071 *601 Squadron* in March 1966. *Geoff Rixon*

Above: One unrebuilt light Pacific, No 34064 *Fighter Command*, was experimentally fitted with a Giesl in-line ejector chimney. The locomotive is seen passing Farnborough with a morning Waterloo-Bournemouth/ Weymouth express on 9 September 1962. *Rodney Lissenden*

Right: The 1.30pm from Waterloo to Bournemouth thunders through Fleet behind rebuilt 'Merchant Navy' 4-6-2 No 35003 *Royal Mail. Hugh Ballantyne*

Above: BR Standard '5' 4-6-0 No 73113 *Lyonnesse* works hard near Brookwood with a summer Saturday extra from Waterloo to Swanage. The rectangular board tied to the smokebox door carries a special Saturday train reporting number to ease the lot of signalmen in identifying trains. *Derek Cross*

Right: Rebuilt No 34008 *Padstow* pounds up the 1 in 252 gradient from Eastleigh, near Allbrook, with an up Bournemouth-Waterloo express on 10 July 1964. *Les Elsey*

Left: Near the end of steam on the Southern standards of locomotive presentation began to slip. Seen waiting for the 'right away' at Southampton Central *en route* for Bournemouth is 'Merchant Navy No 35013 *Blue Funnel Certum Pete Finem* minus nameplates. *Alan Wild*

Right: Deep in the New Forest, unrebuilt 'West Country' 4-6-2 No 34023 *Blackmore Vale* (sadly shorn of its nameplates) climbs between Lymington Junction and Sway with a down Waterloo-Bournemouth train on 25 March 1966. *Alan Trickett*

Left: No 34095 *Brentor* heads through Christchurch with a Bournemouth-bound express. *G. W. Morrison*

Below left: Watched by the inevitable interested observer, 'Merchant Navy' 4-6-2 No 35012 *United States Lines* calls at Bournemouth Central with the up 'Bournemouth Belle' Pullman train for Southampton and London on 24 May 1959. *Colin Boocock*

Right: In the calm and leafy suburbs of west Bournemouth, 'Merchant Navy' 4-6-2 No 35021 *New Zealand Line* approaches the Gas Works Junction split distant signal; the signal is set to route the down 'Bournemouth Belle' to its destination at Bournemouth West.
G. W. Morrison

Left: In the peaceful terminus of Bournemouth West the main departure of the afternoon awaits the 'right away'. No 35030 *Elder-Dempster Lines* has a full head of steam and a load of probably 12 Pullmans on the up 'Bournemouth Belle'.
Malcolm Knight

Right: Boat trains went to Lymington Pier on Saturdays in the summer to connect with ferries to Yarmouth on the Isle of Wight. These were worked by 'Schools' class 4-4-0s from the time these became displaced by diesels from the Eastern Section of the Southern because they could use the short turntable at Brockenhurst where engines were changed for the Lymington branch 'Q' or 'Q1' 0-6-0. No 30905 *Tonbridge* passes the future location of Southampton Airport (even later, Parkway) station with a down train, carrying the striking headcode and a Saturday reporting number board.
G. W. Morrison

Left: 'Scotch Arthur' No 30795 *Sir Dinadan* has gained a bogie tender and looks smart at the head of an up Greek Line boat train from Southampton Docks to Waterloo on 24 April 1962. *Les Elsey*

Basingstoke and other locals

Left: On the down slow track near Fleet, Maunsell 'S15' No 30833 is seen heading west with a summer Saturday working. Its headcode indicates that the train's destination is Basingstoke. *Hugh Ballantyne*

Right: One of the 'U' class 2-6-0s converted from 'River' 2-6-4Ts, No 31790, heads west past Fleet during 1964 with a local train for Salisbury. *B. J. Swain*

Above: 'King Arthur' 4-6-0 No 30798 *Sir Hectimere* passes Weybridge with an up local from Basingstoke in 1962. *Geoff Rixon*

Right: No 73119 *Elaine* near Fleet with a down Basingstoke local train in 1964. The use of second-hand non-corridor BR standard stock on these trains was not a regular feature in the editor's experience. *B. J. Swain*

Above: Drummond's large 'D15' class 4-4-0s, like No 30465 pictured here, spent some useful years working the Basingstoke and other local trains, until their demise in late 1950s. *Stephen Townroe/Colour-Rail*

Right: 'N' class 2-6-0 No 31869 passes 'Q1' 0-6-0 No 33037 outside Basingstoke on 24 August 1962. The 2-6-0 was arriving with a local from Waterloo. *Alan Trickett*

Left: Having called at Andover for custom, BR Standard '4' 4-6-0 No 75075 awaits the 'right away' with a Waterloo-Salisbury stopping train on 19 April 1967. *G. S. Cocks*

Empty stock and service workings

Right: Until modern carriage workings introduced the concept of speedy turnrounds in the terminus stations, most steam-hauled trains which arrived at Waterloo were taken to Clapham Junction carriage sidings for cleaning and servicing before their next down working. 'M7' 0-4-4T No 30320 is in charge of one such empty stock working as it passes West London Junction in June 1961. *J. Oatway*

Above: An overall view of Clapham carriage sheds showing BR Standard '3' 2-6-2T No 82019 shunting vans on 20 May 1967. Locomotive-hauled and multiple-unit stock is on view. *Douglas Hume*

Right: No 82019 is seen again, this time taking its train of vans onto the Kensington line at Clapham Junction. *Douglas Hume*

Above: 'T9' 4-4-0 No 30719 takes a civil engineers' ballast cleaner through the cutting near Brookwood. *Derek Cross*

Right: The presence of Drummond '700' class 0-6-0 No 30694 at Nine Elms in April 1959 suggests that it has just delivered a train of locomotive coal *T. J. Edgington/Colour-Rail*

Left: Depot shunting locomotives at Nine Elms were often former London, Brighton & South Coast Railway 'E4' class 0-6-2Ts such as No 32487 seen here. *G. W. Morrison*

Above: Other freight in the London area on the Waterloo main line was very limited in quantity. In this view a Urie 'H16' class 4-6-2T, No 30518, passes Weybridge with coal for the power station at Durnsford Road, Wimbledon. *Geoff Rixon*

Left: Maunsell 'N' class 2-6-0 No 31811 heads west out of Woking yard with a freight on 25 July 1964. *G. S. Cocks*

Specials

Right: Railtours in the 1960s brought steam locomotives (not necessarily preserved ones) into new or unfamiliar surroundings. Yet these two Beattie well tanks, Nos 30585 and 30587, seen approaching Wimbledon in December 1962 on an enthusiasts' railtour, had been used on suburban workings in the area late in the 19th century! They had spent their last few decades working clay wagons on the Wenfordbridge branch in Cornwall. *J. P. Mullett*

Above: An unusual visiting locomotive to a depot such as Nine Elms always attracted an interested crowd. Preserved 'A3' 4-6-2 No 4472 *Flying Scotsman* stands among the Bulleid locomotives at Nine Elms on 29 May 1965 before setting off on a special. *Rodney Lissenden*

Right: Even though they were still relatively regular performers on the main line, unrebuilt Bulleid light Pacifics were popular for railtours in the mid-1960s. 'West Country' No 34102 (formerly named *Lapford*) leads 'Battle of Britain' sister No 34057 *Biggin Hill* on a railtour to Bridport in Dorset. They were photographed during a stop at Grateley on 22 January 1967. *Alan Trickett*

Above: Ivatt 2-6-0 No 46509 was unusual power for the Locomotive Club of Great Britain's Thames Valley Railtour. The locomotive is seen being prepared outside the 'new shed' at Nine Elms on Sunday 25 July 1965. *G. S. Cocks*

Right: Seen in absolutely resplendent condition, 'A2' Pacific No 60532 *Blue Peter* pulls out from under the Nine Elms coaling plant prior to working the LCGB 'A2 Commemorative Tour' on 14 August 1966. *G. S. Cocks*

Above: Unusual interest would have been taken in the appearance on the Southern of Gresley three-cylinder 2-6-0 No 3442 *The Great Marquess* when it worked a railtour from Victoria to Brighton and Portsmouth on 12 March 1967. Here it shares the Nine Elms scene with a BR Standard '3' 2-6-2T. *G. S. Cocks*

Right: Police are on hand at Waterloo to ensure order as enthusiasts see preserved 'A4' Pacific No 4498 *Sir Nigel Gresley* ready to leave with an A4 Society special on 3 June 1967. Electro-diesel Bo-Bo No E6014 stands alongside, probably with a Weymouth Quay boat train. *G. S. Cocks*

The last days of BR main line steam

Left: The lack of recruitment of locomotive cleaners in the last year of Southern steam left many Pacific locomotives looking sad and dishevelled. This is No 34024 (formerly *Tamar Valley*) calling at Basingstoke on 7 July 1967. *Douglas Hume*

Right: Prior to hauling one of the last official steam specials, No 35008 is shunted under the coaling plant at Nine Elms by Ivatt 2-6-2T No 41319. *G. S. Cocks*

Left: The second official last steam train, the 4.30pm from Bournemouth to Waterloo, passes Pokesdown in the Bournemouth suburbs, headed by 'Merchant Navy' No 35028 *Clan Line* on 2 July 1967. *Hugh Ballantyne*

Above: As steam runs down, Basingstoke shed is almost completely empty in June 1967, apart from No 34102 resting outside and now without its *Lapford* nameplates. *Geoff Rixon*

Epilogue

Above: On the last day of steam, 9 July 1967, Nine Elms depot already has an abandoned look. A few steam locomotives stand in a desultory fashion outside the demolished 'old shed'. The 'new shed' on the right looks almost empty. Some bystanders look on. By the next day all the locomotives will have been rounded up and taken away to Salisbury for storage prior to scrapping. *G. S. Cocks*

Appendix 1

70A Locomotive allocation at 31 August 1950

Class M7 0-4-4T

30038	30123	30130	30132	30241
30244	30248	30249	30319	30322
30667	30676			

Class T9 4-4-0

30119   30718

Class G6 0-6-0T

30160   30259   30353

Class L11 4-4-0

30163   30165   30405   30406

Class O2 0-4-4T

30221

Class H15 4-6-0

30332	30333	30334	30335	30476
30482	30484	30485	30486	30487
30488	30490			

Class 700 0-6-0

30339   30692   30694   30699   30701

Class K10 4-4-0

30390

Class T14 4-6-0

30446   30461

Class N15 'King Arthur' 4-6-0

30742 *Camelot*	30745 *Tintagel*
30747 *Elaine*	30755 *The Red Knight*
30765 *Sir Gareth*	30773 *Sir Lavaine*
30780 *Sir Persant*	30782 *Sir Brian*
30787 *Sir Menadeuke*	30791 *Sir Uwaine*
30792 *Sir Hervis de Revel*	

Class LN 'Lord Nelson' 4-6-0

30858 *Lord Duncan*	30859 *Lord Hood*
30860 *Lord Hawke*	

Class Z 0-8-0T

30955

Class H 0-4-4T

31551   31552   31553   31554

Class U 2-6-0

31613   31619   31625   31637   31807

Class E1 0-6-0T

32138

Class E4 0-6-2T

32468   32493   32500

Class BB 'Battle of Britain' 4-6-2

34049 *Anti-Aircraft Command*
34050 *Royal Observer Corps*
34051 *Winston Churchill*   34052 *Lord Dowding*
34053 *Sir Keith Park*
34054 *Lord Beaverbrook*   34055 *Fighter Pilot*
34056 *Croydon*   34057 *Biggin Hill*
34058 *Sir Frederick Pile*
34059 *Sir Archibald Sinclair*
34060 *25 Squadron*   34061 *73 Squadron*
34062 *17 Squadron*   34063 *229 Squadron*
34064 *Fighter Command*   34065 *Hurricane*

Class MN 'Merchant Navy' 4-6-2

35005 *Canadian Pacific*   35010 *Blue Star*
35011 *General Steam Navigation*
35012 *United States Lines*
35013 *Blue Funnel Certum Pete Finem*
35014 *Nederland Line*
35015 *Rotterdam Lloyd*   35016 *Elders Fyffes*
35017 *Belgian Marine*
35018 *British India Line*
35019 *French Line CGT*   35020 *Bibby Line*

Total 99

Appendix 2

70A Locomotive allocation in 1959

Class 57xx 0-6-0PT

4634	4672	4686	4692	4698
9770				

Class M7 0-4-4T

30123	30133	30241	30245	30248
30249	30319	30320	30321	

Class T9 4-4-0

30338   30718   30719

Class N15 'King Arthur' 4-6-0

30457 *Sir Bedivere*	30763 *Sir Bors de Ganis*
30774 *Sir Gaheris*	30778 *Sir Pelleas*
30779 *Sir Colgrevance*	

Class H15 4-6-0

30482	30484	30486	30489	30491
30521	30522	30523	30524	

Class 700 0-6-0

30694   30699   30701

Class V 'Schools' 4-4-0

30902 *Wellington*	30903 *Charterhouse*
30906 *Sherborne*	30907 *Dulwich*

Class U 2-6-0

31617   31621   31624   31634   31796

Class E4 0-6-2T

32487   32497   32498   32500   32563

Class Q1 0-6-0

33015   33017   33038

Class WC 'West Country' 4-6-2

34006 *Bude*	34007 *Wadebridge*
34009 *Lyme Regis*	34010 *Sidmouth*
34018 *Axminster*	34020 *Seaton*
34029 *Lundy*	34031 *Torrington*
34047 *Callington*	34093 *Saunton*
34094 *Mortehoe*	34095 *Brentor*

Class BB 'Battle of Britain' 4-6-2

34064 *Fighter Command*	34065 *Hurricane*
34090 *Sir Eustace Missenden, Southern Railway*	

Class MN 'Merchant Navy' 4-6-2

35005 *Canadian Pacific*
35012 *United States Lines*
35014 *Nederland Line*   35016 *Elders Fyffes*
35017 *Belgian Marine*
35018 *British India Line*
35019 *French Line CGT*   35020 *Bibby Line*
35029 *Ellerman Lines*
35030 *Elder-Dempster Lines*

BR Standard '5' 4-6-0

73087 *Linette*	73088 *Joyous Gard*
73089 *Maid of Astolat*	73110 *The Red Knight*
73111 *King Uther*	73112 *Morgan le Fay*
73113 *Lyonnesse*	73114 *Etarre*
73115 *King Pellinore*	73116 *Iseult*
73117 *Vivien*	
73118 *King Leodegrance*	
73119 *Elaine*	

Total 90

Note: Not all the BR Standard '5' 4-6-0s had received their names in 1959.

Appendix 3
70A Locomotive allocation at 25 October 1965

Class Q1 0-6-0
33006   33020   33027

Class WC 'West Country' 4-6-2
34001 *Exeter*   34002 *Salisbury*
34021 *Dartmoor*   34038 *Lynton*

BR Standard '5' 4-6-0
73086 *The Green Knight*

BR Standard '4' 2-6-4T
80012   80015   80069   80095   80133
80137   80143   80154

BR Standard '3' 2-6-2T
82006   82018   82019   82023   82024
82026   82027   82028   82029

Total 25

Right: A row of water columns stands like a line of wounded sentinels at the end of 70A depot's useful life. *G. S. Cocks*